LIV'N
THE
SCOUT LAW

The Foundation to your Success

JUSTEN A. KAYSE

WESTBOW
PRESS®
A DIVISION OF THOMAS NELSON
& ZONDERVAN

This book is a work of non-fiction. Unless otherwise noted, the author
and the publisher make no explicit guarantees as to the accuracy of
the information contained in this book and in some cases, names of
people and places have been altered to protect their privacy.

WestBow Press books may be ordered through booksellers or by contacting:

WestBow Press
A Division of Thomas Nelson & Zondervan
1663 Liberty Drive
Bloomington, IN 47403
www.westbowpress.com
844-714-3454

ISBN: 978-1-6642-7700-7 (sc)
ISBN: 978-1-6642-7701-4 (hc)
ISBN: 978-1-6642-7699-4 (e)

Library of Congress Control Number: 2022916160

Print information available on the last page.

WestBow Press rev. date: 09/29/2022

CONTENTS

Acknowledgments.. ix

Introduction xiii

Chapter 1   Trustworthy.. 1

Chapter 2   Loyal.. 9

Chapter 3   Helpful... 15

Chapter 4   Friendly.. 23

Chapter 5   Courteous 27

Chapter 6   Kind.. 33

Chapter 7   Obedient.. 39

Chapter 8   Cheerful.. 51

Chapter 9   Thrifty 57

Chapter 10 Brave... 63

Chapter 11 Clean 71

Chapter 12 Reverent.. 77

Chapter 13 And Always Hungry 85

Conclusion 89

About the Author... 105

.

I wrote this book in memory of my parents. They both led hundreds if not thousands of boys and girls through the scouting program. The scouting world was a big part of their lives, and they inspired many young people to become amazing people. I say to them, "Thank you for giving me and so many others such a great experience and guidance that led me through life from a child to a man and will forever more. I love you both, and thank you from the bottom of my heart."

My dad, a commissioner in scouting, earning several leadership awards. He was a silver-beaver award recipient as well as a vigil honor in the Order of the Arrow. The Boy Scouts of America honored my father for his dedication to scouting with the Lobo Memorial Award.

My mom was a recipient of numerous den mother of the year awards in Boy Scouts and troop leader in Girl Scouts.

A special thank you to my dad for showing me daily how to use the scout law and to treat others and lead with respect. Dad showed his best with his respect for my mother every day. Showing small gestures of appreciation were sometimes the biggest gifts of all, like building a swing for my mother so they could sit together and watch the sunsets over Biggby Lake. Many times, I watched them sit on the swing, enjoying each other's company as the sun set.

I will always be grateful for these memories and for the things I've learned. Thank you for sparking the fire that lives within me each and every day I live.

Love you both.

ACKNOWLEDGMENTS

To begin, I'd like to thank my parents for ultimately getting me involved with scouting. Even though I fought it in the beginning, it was one of the best things for me to grow up with in my life. When I meet people who weren't in scouting, the lack of things they know about amazes me.

To the scout leaders I had over the years and the fathers of boys who came on camping trips and added their two cents wherever they thought fit, it helped. Thank you!

Thank you to the Boy Scouts of America for being so structured and informative. Through the scouts, I learned to be not just a survivor in this thing we call life but a seeker of better things in this journey we travel. And to all the scouts who made something out of themselves and inspired me to be more, thank you.

To all the motivational speakers who encouraged me to go for it, thank you.

And a special thank you goes to Rebecca Hamilton for doing an amazing job on the artwork in this book. I literally get goosebumps when I see your work in the pages of my book. To anyone that wants artwork from Rebecca Hamilton, go to Oh my Soul Art on Facebook or Instagram, or visit her website, www.ohmysoulart.com.

To my family and friends, who inspired me to stay focused on my dreams and never give up, thank you. And to the love of my life, my wife. Thank you for not giving up on me through all these years. I love you; you are my four-leaf clover.

Finally, thank you to all the wonderful people picking up and reading my book. I thank you for giving me a chance to inspire you, and I encourage you to keep pushing on and moving forward. You are obviously looking to better yourself, and I commend you for it. Stay true to yourself. If you ever need anything, I'm an email away.

INTRODUCTION

As a young boy, I couldn't imagine going to those boring ole scouting events. My dad would leave on a Friday and go camping or take off one evening for the weekly meetings—a guy's club I guessed—and I never felt like it was my cup of tea. In my eyes, it was like my parents were trying to force me to join this thing, and I wasn't going to budge an inch. I refused with a temper tantrum, a foot stomp, and a mean march to my room until they finally gave up.

Weeks later, some scouts came walking into our third-grade classroom. They gave a slide show of the fun things they did and told us things we could learn. My best friends in class were all geeked about joining. And that, my friends, was how it all began. In a blink of an eye, I was in. These older, wiser boys from a few classes higher sold me on a new lifestyle way better than my parents ever did. Obviously, the slide show did it.

I went home all excited about the new adventure. And when I told my parents I wanted to join the scouts, the looks on their faces was priceless.

The Boy Scout slogan is, "Do a good turn daily."

The Boy Scout motto is, "Be Prepared."

The Boy Scout oath is:

On my honor, I will do my best to do my duty to God and my country and to obey the scout law; to help other people at all times; to keep myself physically strong, mentally awake and morally straight.

These items I've spoken of—the oath, the slogan, and the motto—are very powerful things that will change your life in positive ways. I'll break them down for you, but you'll have to wait as I'll include these powerful features in my next book, *Liv'n the Scout Oath*. Look for it as it will be the next game-changer book for you to read. For now, let's cover the scout law and how it is the base of the foundation to success.

The Boy Scout law is:

A Scout is Trustworthy, Loyal, Helpful, Friendly, Courteous, Kind, Obedient, Cheerful, Thrifty, Brave, Clean, and Reverent.

Oh, and always hungry. Hungry is an unofficial addition by every scout who ever lived.

Ladies and gentlemen, "Success is in the eye of the beholder." Oh, wait. That is wrong. It is, "Beauty is in the eye of the beholder," right? Or does it work both ways? "Success is in the eye of the beholder." Yes, I think it does, and that is why having a foundation like the Boy Scout law works so well.

In this book I break down all these things and tell you how they can help you in your daily life. I share my personal experiences or those of someone worthy of the story being told. By following these steps, you can become a very successful person. I cannot tell you that every boy who was in Boy Scouts became successful. As you know, we all follow different paths. There may be forks in the road of life, and some of us—even Boy Scouts—take a wrong turn.

But unless you live under a rock, you might recognize a few former scouts who took the path less traveled and used the scouting foundation as a platform to catapult themselves into a successful life. I want to be clear; I'm not name-dropping, but I'm name-dropping. So let's make this fun and get your mind thinking a little. One of the best ways to be successful is to exercise the mind as well as the body. And the best way to do that, besides reading, are brain games, so as you read this chapter, I'll test your abilities, giving you clues, and you can fill in the blanks to get the answers. If push comes to shove and you don't know the answer, there is always the World Wide Web to help you out. If you're a basketball fan like me, you might recognize the famous basketball player who could fly like an eagle. His nickname included nothing more than air, and he owns his own brand, with the logo being himself, on all his shoes and outerwear. M_ _ _ _ _ L _ _ _ _ _N took the sports route and became a pretty good ball handler. OK, a great ball handler in his day. He mastered the game like no one else, and in many people's eyes, he is still considered the all-time greatest. Do you know this former Boy Scout?

Maybe you're more into comedy and acting, like this next guy. Have you been schooled in rock and roll, or are you more of a board game kind of person, living inside the game? Whatever you choose, just don't be shallow around J_ _ _ B_ _ _ _. Trust me when I tell you there are plenty of former scouts in the acting business, and that is probably because in scouts, it wasn't uncommon to do skits around a campfire.

Another funny guy on the big screen would be none other than C_ _ _ _ _ r_ _ _, a former guardian of us all and a huge recreation fan in the parks. Can you name this scout?

Maybe you prefer a more serious actor, one who plays a tomb raider to a doctor on the run. H_ _ _ I _ _ _ F_ _ _ has gone from treasure hunter to president and back. From Mr. Romantic to fugitive on the run, he has amazed the us all with his talents as a great actor. I've only gave you bits and pieces just to name a few. But let's not forget film directors, like M_ _ _ _ _ _ M_ _ r_, a well-known documentarian from the Great Lake state. His films can be controversial, but that is what makes him so interesting and eye-opening as a filmmaker.

Mr. _ _ _v_ _p_ _ _ _ _ _ _, on the other hand, has directed some of the greatest films on the big screen today. He is considered the most commercially successful director of all times. I had the pleasure of meeting him in 1988 at a national jamboree in Virginia. It was amazing to see a great guy giving back to scouting by taking time away from his work to help teach a merit badge. J _ _ _ L_ _ _ g _w's passion for acting was ignited by being a Boy Scout. He then studied his craft at a well-acclaimed university and arts school. Then it was on to Broadway to start his career on stage and then the big screen. He has earned many awards for his great performances throughout the years.

If you like music, you probably know the famous "Margaritaville" man. _ _ mm _ _ _ ff _ _ has used some of the skills he learned as a Boy Scout, including a few helpful first aid skills he has used on numerous occasions.

Personally, I like when it rains, and you see lightning and hear thunder. Speaking of thunder, how about the band that performs that song. The lead singer _ _ n R _ y _ _ _ _ _ is also a songwriter. The band has won many awards as well as been on top of the *Billboard* charts in the music industry. D _ _ was not just in scouting. He received the highest honor, earning his Eagle Scout award.

But hey, some of you prefer to be techies or politicians, so I better let you in on one of the largest tech companies' cofounders, _ _ ll _ _ t _ _. He achieved the rank of Life, and the Boy Scouts of America awarded him the Silver Buffalo award in 2010 for his service to the youth. Mr. _ _ t _ _ is not only a successful software developer but an avid investor, author, and philanthropist.

If that guy didn't excite you, maybe we should strap you to a rocket and send you to the moon like Eagle scouts N_ _ _ A _ _ _ _ _ _ _ _ or _ _ _ z A_ _ _ _ _. If I didn't just hit that one out of the park, then I'll let Boy Scout Hammering H_ _ _ A _ _ _ _ do it for me.

I'm pretty sure that by now, I've made my point, and I don't have to mention other great Americans, like Baptist minister and civil rights activist _ _ _ t _ _ _ _ t _ _ _ K _ _ _ Jr. Or how about our thirty-fifth president J _ _ _ F. K _ _ _ _ _ _? I'll just move on singing a country tune from my buddy, fellow Boy Scout G _ _ _ _ S _ _ _ _ _. Not only a great singer, songwriter, and music producer, but also an actor. He is known as the pioneer of neotraditional country. If you can't find him on the big stage singing a song, you'll find him on his property being a rancher. Hats off to this veteran and CMA winner.

I don't have to tell you that scouting was a big part of these guys' lives. But everything in their lives started from the foundation of scouting. They chose to expand on it and became who they are today.

I start with the scout law, but as you'll see, to be a good, all-around scout and person, you need more than just the law. You need the Boy Scout oath, motto, and slogan to be complete, and you'll find that part in my sequel, *Liv'n the Scout Oath*.

Every day we all make choices to follow or not follow the Boy Scout law, oath, and motto. You can reflect on choices you've made, and see if they were positive moves or if they set you up to go backwards in life. I always tell people, "Always and forever forward in what you do." Or ask yourself, "WWFMD"—"What would future me do?" That is where the foundation of scouting can really play a role in your life. In life we should ask ourselves this every day and make choices that help us to move forward. Using the Boy Scout law as a foundation will help you make these decisions. Let's begin, shall we?

CHAPTER 1

Trustworthy

Trust-wor-thy: able to be relied on as an honest or truthful person; deserving of trust or confidence; dependable; reliable.

A SCOUT IS TRUSTWORTHY

In life, being trustworthy can be as simple as being a person others can count on to perform a task, such as picking up milk on the way home from work. Or you might give a trustworthy neighbor kid your house key and ask him or her to water the plants and get your mail. A Secret Service agent or an ambassador of a country can be trusted to keep top-secret things to themselves. Being trustworthy is as simple as that.

I remember a time we were camping on Long Island on Short Lake in the middle of winter. On Sunday, our departure day, a heavy winter storm blew in with over seventy-one-mile-per-hour winds. We were supposed to hike off the island and back to the mainland in a storm that was blowing snow sideways. Snow was falling inches per hour, so fast you couldn't see the guy standing in front of you. Mind you, this was before cell phones, back in the mid-1980s.

As kids, we wholeheartedly trusted our adult scout leaders to get us home safely. I remember our leaders got out rope and had us all hold on to it, so we all knew where everyone was, and no one would get separated. Now my dad did not stay at this outing, so the trust I had was solely on other Boy Scout dads, who were our leaders on this trip.

Of course, leave it to Jay and I to cross-country ski to the island, so we had to strap in and ski back. Let me tell you, the wind tried its best to take us away. Mr. Adams, Pete's dad, was leading us to the mainland. It didn't take long for us to realize we were on a lake, with no sight of land in front of or behind us. The wind whipped us around like rag dolls, and it was impossible to see. Mr. Adams stopped us maybe three hundred yards away from the island, grouped us up, and made a new plan to head back to Long Island before we wouldn't know where it was. His call to turn us back knowing we still had food to last another day or two was the smartest thing to do. As kids, we probably would've tried to continue, and who knows what could've happened. Some boys were a little scared. Others were thinking we'd just gotten out of going to school on Monday.

Once back to the cabin on the island, we set our gear down and built a fire to stay warm. We knew we were safe, and our families knew where we were. Unfortunately, they knew we were supposed to leave that island, and they were wondering why we hadn't come to shore yet, not being able to communicate. On the mainland, parents went into action. Without our knowledge, the fire department, which had fellow scouts on it, and my father prepared to rescue us with snowmobiles. The plan was brought together with three snowmobiles and a handful of volunteers to ride out from the boat launch straight to the island. There, they would load up a scout and bring him to shore, going back and forth till all scouts were back on the mainland.

This was a great plan, as the snowmobiles weighed enough not to be blown around by the extremely high winds. The only problem was visibility, which they learned once they got moving. They found themselves in a complete whiteout, missed the island, and ended up on the other side of the lake. Given how long the island is and how directly in front of the boat launch it is, I cannot tell you how that is even possible, but they missed it. One ended up a mile down the lake and another in the other direction, losing a volunteer who fell off the sled and broke his glasses on the ice doing so. But one sled made it to the island. How long it took, I'm not sure, but the volunteer said he caught the shoreline and ended up driving along it until he found the cabin. He was stumped that the other sleds hadn't made it there yet. They had to revamp the plan some and try to find a better solution.

We heard noises from outside the cabin and saw another snowmobile had arrived. Now there was only one missing. Most likely it was the one that missed the island to the south side. Not being one to wear a watch, I'd have to say it was hours before the other snowmobile showed up. They realized they'd missed the island and then found the opposite shoreline. They decided the best way to get back was to follow the shoreline all the way around the lake back to the boat launch. By the time they got to the launch, the first snowmobile had already brought a fellow scout over by following the island to the end and then shooting across to a point on the mainland that was closer than the boat launch. Then he followed the shoreline to the launch. The revised plan was a success, and the plan to use the point, as it was the shortest distance, was a go.

The second snowmobile that arrived up to the island carried my dad. He was a little bruised up from a fall on the ice when the driver made a quick turn to miss an ice shanty. Yes, my dad was the one with the broken glasses and a cut above one eye. Larry was the driver of that sled, and he was always a wild one from the stories I'd heard from my older brothers. His brother Darrel was the driver of the first sled that had shown up. Their plan worked, and over the next few hours, they got everyone off the island safely. And sadly, every boy made it to school on Monday morning.

Trust obviously came into play in multiple areas of this story, with the scouts trusting their leader and volunteers to get them safely off the island and lake. Parents trusted that the leaders and volunteers would take care of their kids and return them safely.

Another common example of trust that probably gets overlooked easily can be something as simple as your employer trusting you to deliver a customer's goods across the country because you work for him. The customer hired him and trusted that my boss hired me to drive a semitruck across country to deliver the household goods. Why? Because I worked for a moving company back in the late nineties, and that was my job—to be trusted to move people's lives from one location to another. I had to earn complete strangers' trust on a daily basis for my job. When I worked for Speedy Brothers Moving Company in Cadillac, Michigan, they trusted me to drive the biggest moving trucks they owned, and I trusted they would pay me well. During this time, besides our trust among ourselves, I had to gain the customers' trust because if they felt unsafe giving me their worldly possessions, then I'd get fired.

One time I was asked to deliver a chair from the East Coast to Texas. Bada bing, bada boom, and it was done. I delivered it because that was what we were hired to do. Little did I know that chair was just a test-run delivery by one person to another. And now I had a guy asking me to deliver a chair back to the East Coast but with an envelope attached to the job—a little extra incentive to get the job done. I must admit this threw me for a loop. I mean, I've encountered a few things in my days of driving trucks that didn't seem ethical, and this was one of those times when my gut was uneasy. I'll tell you, this envelope with money stuffed inside to a single guy in his early twenties seemed like a nice bonus, but I declined and went on my way (quickly).

About a week later, another driver, Jack, asked me about it. I thought that was odd. He told me it was a distant relative of his and a family heirloom. Of course, that went through one ear and out the other for me as it seemed to be just like the chair I'd delivered. Jack took the next homeowner's stuff south a week later by request, and I never saw him again. I'd guess he took a chair-transporting job for that relative, or he is at the bottom of a lake tied to a couple cement blocks. In either scenario, I didn't trust the guy in the Texas and, therefore, passed on what could have been a lucrative opportunity.

Obviously, my gut instinct was to walk away because it was illegal, dangerous, and not what I signed up for, heirloom or not.

Obviously, the moral of these stories is trust. Learn to have it in simple things, and build it for the bigger things in life. We must be trustworthy in our daily lives to make a difference and advance in whatever we do.

CHAPTER 2

Loyal

Loy-al: giving or showing firm and constant support or allegiance to a person or institution; the act of being faithful and devoted to someone or something.

A SCOUT IS LOYAL

Loyalty is an act of trust in some form. As far as I see it, when you are loyal to someone, that person has instilled trust in you.

A dog is loyal to its owner. Have you ever seen a dog not happy to see its owner come through the door? Employees can be loyal to their bosses and the companies they work for simply by showing up and doing their jobs every day. I know my dad was loyal to his boss and the automotive body shop he worked for through thick and thin for more than forty years.

Today, you don't often see or hear of that kind of loyalty in the workplace. People are always trying to better themselves, hopping from one employer to the next, advancing as they go. From what I've noticed, it doesn't seem that businesses try hard enough to keep people long term. Many businesses have given up on loyalty plans and use people until they can find new, younger, and cheaper people to fill the slots. It is almost shameful to watch. The government is making it even tougher on them to retain employees with a bazillion taxes and rules to follow regarding benefits. Instead of letting businesses handle things, the government tries to control them.

But we're not here to talk about them and all that deep, depressing kind of stuff. We're here to be positive about how we can better ourselves with our own loyalty plans. People can relate to loyalty by simply looking to their friends or maybe a family member, one you can trust. When people get older, they get married and become loyal to their spouses in sickness and in health, for richer or poorer. You take an oath to be loyal to that special someone in your life. When you see professional athletes, award-winning actors, and bands that made the big time, you'll see all kinds of loyalty, including fans going to a concert or game. Even the professionals themselves are loyal to themselves and stay true to their dreams and goals, eventually making it to the big time.

Loyalty is easy to find if you flip on the radio or click on a television set. Do you have a favorite TV show? Do you watch it every week? There you go; you are loyal to that show.

I grew up in a house with some baseball fans; my oldest brother, Bill, is a huge baseball fan. If I remember correctly, he has always collected baseball cards and watched every baseball game. If it wasn't available on television, he would sit in the dining room with his ear pressed to the radio, listening to the game on the radio station, never missing a pitch. He knew everything that happened in every game with every player. Bill kept precise track of every pitch and every hit of each player. He could tell you if someone was out sick or if their wives were having a baby. If something was going on with his favorite team, even if it was in the upper management, he would know. Bill could name all the current and past players. And now, forty years later, he is still as loyal as day one. He loves his baseball.

Being loyal to your favorite team or player is sometimes as loyal as one person can get. I have another friend, Joel, who was in scouting with me. He is one funny guy and an amazing chef. We kind of drifted apart for many years after school, as so many people do with careers and so forth.

Joel became an amazing chef and won cooking competitions all over the United States. During some point in his life, he ate the food he went to school to learn how to make. He became a foodie, and it got away from him. Joel gained weight over some years and became a chunky monkey. He wanted to change, and his doctors said he needed to change and to do what he needed to be loyal to himself and create goals and a new lifestyle. And boy, when Joel takes on a challenge and his life depends on it, look out! He is unstoppable. Joel not only lost weight and got fit, he got buff and won a muscle-modeling contest. The loyalty he had to himself to beat obesity and laugh in its face blew my mind.

And that was only the beginning. He knew nothing was impossible and that was when he found himself on a food podcast and became a champion chef. Joel is a true hero to so many of us. And if you get a chance to meet him and try his cooking, I say, "Go west," because for now, that is where her has landed as a chef instructor, BBQ competitor, and owner of Chow Thyme BBQ. And let's not forget food podcast, *Champion Chef.*

You don't have to be a former or current Boy Scout to have loyalty. You do, however, have to be committed to what you believe in. Be committed to your goals, and most of all, be committed to the journey because that is where the blood and sweat happen, not the finish line. You'll realize in life that the goal is to get you to experience the journey to the result—your goal, the dream. You need to realize the goal is a benchmark or a notch for you to reach, celebrate, and move on to the next one. So many people stop once they get to the goal, but that is only the finish line for one journey. Our lives are made of many journeys, many goals. Be loyal to yourself and your goals, but most important, be loyal to the journey it brings you through.

CHAPTER 3

Helpful

Help-ful: giving or ready to give help.

Helpful is someone or something that is prone to providing aid.

A SCOUT IS HELPFUL

I think helpful is self-explanatory. The key is how much help you give. If you want something in life, you must first give something. I know half of you are thinking, *Here we go. Be a giver, and it will boomerang back to times ten.* And the other half of you are rolling your eyes and thinking, *Duh. Karma is a nightmare!*

Let me digress. Back in the late 1970s, my family was camping in the north woods of the UP. I was a young boy back then, maybe four years old. Let me back up a slight bit and explain that the UP is the upper peninsula of Michigan I believe we were camping in the Marquette area to visit my sisters, who were going to school at the university there.

One fall day, the sun was shining, and the breeze was cool. My parents told me to put my shoes on and get ready because we were going to explore the mighty U.P. So I put my shoes on, but there was no tying them. I was only four and didn't know how. My parents told me if I did not learn to tie my shoes, I could not go sightseeing. I stormed into our little pop-up camper and sat and pouted like any little kid would. Bill came into the camper and told me, "Today you learn how to tie your shoes." He told our parents to go on without us, and he'd stay and teach me how to tie my shoes.

He told me to come out of the camper. He sat me on top of the picnic table, and for what seemed like hours after hours, he showed me over and over how to tie my shoes. And by the time everyone came back from sightseeing, I knew how to tie my shoes. Now granted, I told him it'd be easier if they had sticky laces that I could just fold over nice and tight, and it'd hold until I decided to undo them. But he said that didn't exist, only string, and I was gonna learn the rabbit trick. Yes, I'm pretty sure I invented Velcro at age four. Too bad I didn't patent it.

Every time I sit and think about that time, how despite the fact the weather was perfect for camping and sightseeing, my brother had so much patience with me that day. Over and over, I failed to get it right, and he never stopped showing me the correct way until it was cemented into my brain. I realize now that teaching me how to tie my shoes helped both of us. I became more self-efficient, and Bill didn't have to hear my parents yell at me for not doing it. Our departure times were always delayed by my lack of knowledge. My brother's kindness and willingness to help me created a chain effect. He not only helped himself by helping me, he also helped my parents and my sisters. And I now realize this chain effect as I teach my kids how to tie their shoes.

I remember the time my dad, my scout troop, and I were camping in Brevort, a small fishing town in the UP. A shout out to Panoramic Trails Council Short Lake Troop 09. What's up, fellow scouters? The time was mid- to late-1980s, and I was a teenager. We left our meeting place at Short Lake Friends Church that Friday and caravanned north to a site near Brevort Lake off Highway 2. I'm not sure of the season, but it was raining and dark by the time we got to the camping area. We went to the wrong campgrounds at first and had to head back out to find the correct one. The camping area was quiet and seemed deserted at that time of night. And with the downpour, it was not the ideal time to set up camp.

We pulled into our campsites, got out, and grouped by the trailer. Everyone knew what to do. It was a grab-and-go kind of thing. We all hustled to get the equipment out of the trailer, and the tents set up in record time. I remember my dad telling me not to worry about us and our tent, just to help everyone else first. We hustled from campsite to campsite, helping fellow scouters set up their tents and get their gear inside as quickly as possible.

Once we got the last tent up, we headed back to our site. Dad said, "We'll just fold down the seats in the station wagon and sleep in the car tonight, so we won't get our gear wet." I almost had to laugh at his suggestion. It was like he was saying, "Enough already. I'm tired of getting wet. Let's get inside, where it's dry." But he did it after helping everyone else first. So we made camp that night in the back of a little, red Nissan station wagon, and it worked out just fine.

When we awoke the next morning, the rain had passed, and the sun was coming up. First off, we built a warm fire with some dry wood we had in the equipment trailer. Dad sent me out to look for other firewood. When I got back, other scouters were making their way out of their tents and gathering by our fire. Dad was giving them all rope to make clotheslines so they could dry out their wet clothing and gear.

I swear every time I turned around, he was helping someone learn something new to make him a better scout and a better person. I've camped with my dad many, many times, and I always learned something new from him. Let me tell you this little tidbit of information. If my dad ever needed help to do something, I don't think anyone ever hesitated to help him. People almost went out of their ways and jumped for an opportunity to help him, trying to pay him back for all the time and help he gave. I can say this: My dad was one class act. That is for sure.

We need to hop in the time machine and zoom to this century. I'll tell you how I took what I've learned about being helpful and, without a blink of an eye, said yes to a dear friend of mine named Archie. Archie is one of my close friends, and a few years back, he started having some medical issues. We thought they were caused by improper medication doses as his doctor just changed them up on him. We were worried about him.

We were on a guys' trip, hundreds of miles from home, when he got sick. Having your friend down and out is scary, to say the least. Once back home, the doctors ran a bunch of tests and found his heart was failing, and he needed a new one soon. Archie went through a lot in the next year just to stay alive. Knowing his life depended on someone else's ending did not sit well with him, which was totally understandable. Archie has a big heart, and I'd do anything for him.

Finally came the day when the phone rang. An out-of-town hospital had a heart for him, and off he went. Within days, he said he felt like a new man. He couldn't believe how well he felt. The doctors said it was because he had been living so long with a bad heart that it was like putting new batteries in a golf cart; it just wants to go, go, go.

There is a lot of maintenance that comes with getting a heart transplant. That requires trips to the hospital weekly for months and a truckload of medications. One of Archie's restrictions was no driving, but he had to go to the hospital weekly, which was two hours away. When you have a new heart, you do what the doc says.

One day my phone rang. It was Archie. He wanted to know if I had Thursdays available and would I drive him to the hospital? Wow! He called me for this task, and I jumped at the opportunity to help my friend. I was honored he asked. I was also happy to see Archie because part of his doctors' orders was to stay home, take it easy, and to make sure to wear face masks. So when I got the green light to help and spend the day with him, I took it. It never crossed my mind to say no or let me check to see if I could. I told him yes immediately. That is part of being a scout—to help people. If you know them or not, be helpful.

I do have to say I joke with Archie all the time that after our road trip together, he begged his doctor to let him drive again because after that visit, the doctor cleared him to drive, and I never got to road trip it to the hospital again. (I probably talked his ear off!) We joke, but every day the doctor lets him do more is progress. And even though I don't get to help him out anymore with car rides, I'm one happy guy to have my friend here, and he is better than ever.

I want to make it clear you don't have to overthink this helping thing and look for big things to help with. It means just as much and is just as important to help with the little things that can pop up every day. I have a neighbor who works a lot to take care of her family. Sometimes it isn't easy to find time to mow the lawn. I have a big lawn mower and enjoy mowing. So if I'm out mowing my yard and see hers needs mowing, I do it, knowing it helps relieve some daily stress on her and checks a to-do off her list. It costs me nothing but means everything to her.

Another small gesture of being a helpful neighbor is going out in the winter and shoveling your neighbor's. walk. Or maybe you see their driveway is slippery, and they walk to the mailbox all the time. So you put some salt on the driveway to make it safer for them. The church I went to as a boy always got the youth group together and cleaned up leaves for the elderly members of the church. Not that they asked, just to do it to help and make their lives a little easier. I have a nephew who lives in the city, and when he sees an elderly person waiting to cross a street, he takes the time to go over and strike up a conversation, and help the person cross the street. Then he goes on with his day. Taking that little bit of time affects people in a positive manner, and it sticks with them. And if you were wondering, yes, my nephew was a Boy Scout.

So you see, helping people can be anything. Even inviting friends, family, or neighbors over for a barbecue so they don't have to cook can be helping them out. And it gives you a chance to catch up and possibly discover other things they might need help with that you can do. We have a friend who is an IT nerd. She has saved our computers more than once. For us, having a computer issue is a major hassle. But for her, it is something she can do in her sleep, so it isn't a big deal to her, but to us it is. So remember, your talents can come in handy in helping people.

Just one last thing. Believe it or not, some people out there love dogs. Sometimes you don't find the time to slow down to walk your dog. You really should take that break because the dog is your therapy. Use your dog; dogs listen. But if you can't find the time, someone will always be happy to walk your puppy around the block. My daughters will in a heartbeat. It makes them happy, your puppy happy, and it helps you out and makes you happy. We all win.

CHAPTER 4

Friendly

Friend-ly: kind and pleasant. The quality or
state of being friendly: such as a disposition to
goodwill, warmth, or kindness to others.

A SCOUT IS FRIENDLY

Making it a point to be friendly is a good practice to get into.
Being friendly is an act of kindness that makes you grow as a
person. And it is contagious.

When you think of being friendly, what comes to mind
first? Who are you friendly with? Why are you friendly with
the people you are friendly to? Most times you are friendly to
people who are friendly to you, your friends, obviously, and
your neighbors, hopefully. I tend to be friendly with everyone
I meet as it may make them more pleasant with me, and that
makes us both happy.

The goal with our friendliness is to get the kindness and
goodwill returned to us and to make someone else's day as

well. My dad always told me to "Kill them with kindness, and you'll have them eating out of your hand."

Let me tell you a story about a man named Jed. Oops, sorry, getting off track. I mean let's go back to my early days as a landscaper. Let's just say you can attract more bears with honey than ham. I literally just made that up. I don't even know what that means; it just came out of me. Let's break it down for fun. The sweeter you are to someone, the more likely that person will be friendly to you. If you are just a ham, you have a 50/50 shot. I don't know if that is the whole picture or just scratching the surface of a bigger picture. But there you have it. Do with it what you like.

I took this to heart with my landscaping business and was always kind to everyone I met. I always went out of my way to ask how people were doing and about their families. And if they had a pet, I'd get its name. Now this is all good only if you remember key facts and use them later. I'd return days later with a bid to do their landscaping. I'd call their pet and any kids I saw by their names. Besides dropping off a bid, I asked how they were doing, and when I went over the bid with them, I used the information they gave me to sell the job. For example, if I saw little Tommy playing cars out in the driveway, I would let them know the patio I would install would make a safer place for Tommy to play cars in the backyard instead of the driveway. People loved that kind of commitment and detail—and that I took the time to know them and be friends rather than just a salesman trying to get the job. Friendliness goes a long way when you add details to it. Making a customer feel like a friend is priceless when it comes to your work environment. Trust me. It doesn't matter what you do or sell, if you make a person feel like a friend, he or she will buy from you every time.

I did a short stint of sales at a local boat shop. Everyone I sold a boat to invited me to join them on the lake. One time I even sold a guy a couple—yes, two side by sides—from the off-roadside of the dealership I worked at because he didn't want to deal with anyone else. He also just happened to be an ex-Nascar driver who lives somewhere in Michigan (I can't say where). One very cool dude, and again someone who invited me to come to their home and hang out, ride side-by-sides, or go out on the boat. How cool is that? And all I was doing was being friendly, nice, kind, and respectful of him and his needs.

Trust me, being friendly is as simple as a smile and a hello. People don't realize how far they can go with just this one law of friendliness. I walk many nature and park trails and always try to smile and greet people with a friendly, "Hello," and a, "Beautiful day for a walk." It makes people smile back, look around, and comment, "Yes, it is." That simple kindness right there could be all it takes to make a person realize life is worth living. And they, in turn, will be likely to greet the next person they see on the trail with a smile and a hello. Being friendly is one of the best chain reactions we have, and it feels good doing it.

CHAPTER 5

Courteous

Cour-te-ous: polite, respectful, or considerate in manner.

A SCOUT IS COURTEOUS

Courteous is something I'm afraid Americans have lost sight of. I mean, they gave up on it and feel that's okay. They think it is just them showing their personalities, and they have that right. But what they don't realize is that personality isn't beneficial! Sorry, not sorry. What they do not realize is that without knowing it, we are branding ourselves each day we expose ourselves to the public. And again without our knowledge, others categorize us as rude. Yep, like it or not, you got tagged. Don't worry; it can change. So if that's you, you still have hope.

Nowadays, you can't leave home without someone being rude and disrespectful to you. I don't even have to leave home for someone to be rude to me, thanks to smartphones.

Being courteous, I guess, is perhaps taught by one's family.

As for being courteous, I can explain to you in many ways that are simple. Good-hearted people just take it for granted. Why? Because they're the ones who were taught to be courteous. They take it for granted that is how it should be. My dad taught me at a young age to always open the door for your lady and the elderly. That seems simple enough to me.

Being courteous is also a form of kindness. Being courteous is letting someone go ahead of you when walking into the store instead of sprinting in front of the person. Being courteous is not talking back to your parents or bosses with attitude. Being courteous is having manners and paying attention. Being courteous is not having your cell phone at the dinner table when you're eating dinner. Being courteous is being present in company. We can easily forget to be courteous with these cell phones attached to us. And that alone is probably one of the biggest sources of rudeness in today's world.

Being courteous is an act toward others that you do out of respect. Cell phones have no respect for people. While their convenience is great, we need to learn to ignore them when we are among company. Courteous is not interrupting others, including by answering your cell phone while someone is talking.

It's time to hop back into that DeLorean and set the time circuits to the year 1994, hit the gas, and cruise to the magical 88 mph, and then head back in time to when I was young and in love (again). Spring was in the air. Ahh, it was a beautiful day, and the night was going to be even better. I'd been planning this day for months, and it had finally arrived. I got all dressed up at my place, a hole-in-the-wall, rundown, 1960s, single-wide, mustard-colored trailer sitting on the side of a hill out in the country, overlooking the best fishing hole in the state of Michigan. Suited up in my finest attire, which I rented, it was time for a hot date with my girlfriend.

I made all the arrangements for it to be a night to remember. It was her senior prom, and one I promised she'd never forget. Earlier that day, I washed and vacuumed my car, put a new air freshener in it. And it was not one of those cheap pine ones but a nice one that smelled like tropical fruit bubblegum. I prepared to woo my girl with as much kindness and courteousness I could. I was pulling out all the stops and chairs.

Everything my dad taught me about being courteous I did. I showed up at her house right on time, which in my dad's book was five minutes early. (Never keep a lady waiting, ever.) Next I ran up to the door, opened it, and walked her to my car. Of course, after her mom and sister took a bazillion pictures of us. I opened the car door for her and shut it after she was safely inside.

I drove to the nicest restaurant I could not afford, but tonight was extra-special, and so was she. and I wanted to make sure she knew it. We pulled up to the Grand Resort. We had reservations at the top of the tower, the Flower Room. I got out of the car, ran around, and opened the door for her. I gave her my hand to help her out, and then I held her hand, and we walked to the front door. Yes, I opened the door for her. I catered to her every need, even if she didn't think it was needed. At the restaurant, I pulled her chair out for her at the table.

After dinner and the dance, I took her for a sunset drive out on Mission Point peninsula to this cute little park. We sat on swings while the sun went down. So did I—on one knee, that is. And right there under the moonlight, I proposed to her, and she said yes. Anyone in an earshot, like the fishermen in the boat just offshore, heard her.

It was a great night of being courteous to someone else. Needless to say, I was courteous and loving for the rest of the night, making my girl feel like a princess. I continued this each and every day after.

Being courteous in one's everyday life is easy to do and quite effortless, and I find it to be needed. I've noticed it's needed the most on the road, when you're driving a car. It is a simple thing to stop at a four-way intersection. and let the other driver go first. Or when going down the road, and someone wants to merge over. Instead of speeding up, try taking your foot off the gas, and let the other driver move over. There seems to be so much road rage out there, and there is no reason for it. Maybe you've been circling a parking lot, looking for a place to park, and some jack rabbit whips into a spot you've been waiting for. Rude! A little common courteous can go a long way, so make sure you're not that jack rabbit, hopping along and stealing parking spots.

CHAPTER 6

Kind

Kind: gracious, kindhearted, kindly. These definitions imply a sympathetic attitude toward others and a willingness to do good or give pleasure. Being kind implies a deep-seated characteristic shown either habitually or on occasion by considerate behavior.

A SCOUT IS KIND

How would you define kind? Do you consider yourself to be kind? Do you know someone who is kind? I mean, say the word, and who pops up in your head? I have many friends who come to mind, but my friend Victor tends to be at the top of the list most often. Victor is the kindest man I know, and believe it or not, I know a lot of people. In fact, I know more than one Victor.

Victor is the guy! He really is. Let me explain why, and you can come up with who among your friends and family stands out as that kind of person. Just to be clear, if any of my other friends are reading this, they know I didn't slight them in any way as they are most likely all nodding in agreement with me that Victor is that guy. Trust me when I say all my friends are kind. It's just that Victor holds the trophy in kindness.

The first time I met Victor was in a bowling alley in mid-Michigan. I walked in just to watch my new friend Bruce bowl with his team, which Victor was on. I had just started dating my wife at the time and was trying to meet some of her friends and hang out in the town more. Bruce found out we had bowling in common and said I should hang out with him one night. I agreed and went to the alley that Wednesday night to watch some bowling and get to know the guys. As soon as I got there, Victor reached out his hand and introduced himself. Then he got me a chair and told me to stay awhile. Ding, ding! First flag of kindness was exposed.

Later that evening, he said, "It looks like you need another drink," and he bought me one. At that moment, I realized this guy was gonna be one of my best friends, not because he bought me some drinks, but because he was such a nice guy and fun to be around. This was my first encounter with Victor's kindness, and I was already impressed.

Encounter number 2 occurred a few months later. I was back in mid-Michigan and gonna sub on the bowling team for one of the other guys. While walking into the bowling alley, I saw Victor on the other side of the parking lot, running to the door. Of course, I assumed he had to go to the bathroom or we were late, and I'm never late. As I looked ahead, I saw some ladies carrying their balls into the alley. Victor slid ahead of them, grabbed the door, and held it open for them. Then he waited for me. My mind was blown. He ran to the door to open it for the ladies. Now mind you, my dad taught me to be a gentleman but never told me I had to run to the door. Victor's kindness and generosity amazed me once again, and we hadn't even gone inside of the bowling center.

We entered together and chatted it up as we walked up the corridor to the bowling lanes. Victor was already cracking some jokes about bowling and that he better get some money out of the ATM for betting the ringer. He was eager to see the bowling skills of the up-north kid—me. Trust me when I say I'm not that good, and most of the time, Victor won my money. But it was all in good fun.

Throughout the night, we all had good laughs and shared in buying some drinks. I noticed Victor was such a gentleman to the wait staff and anyone who walked by, truly showing how kindhearted he was.

Victor became my golf partner that spring, and I can tell you this his kindness based on how he behaved or stories he told never ended. We've been best friends for a while now, and over the years, he has only cemented the kindness with helping hands. After I lost my business to a fire and needed a helping hand, Victor would show up after putting in a long day at his own job and help to get my work done. He would have things prepped for me the next day to keep the momentum going. It didn't matter if he knew how to do something; he wasn't afraid to learn so he could help.

Victor moved a couple hours away, but he still hasn't stopped being kind by any means. So being kind is a lot like being courteous but with more emotion involved.

Kindness isn't strictly meant only for humans. My daughters are kind to every animal they cross paths with, stopping and petting and giving belly rubs to every dog that walks past them. We should practice our kindness with every living thing. Being kind, rather than being rude, to each other makes our lives better and less stressful. A simple smile, hello, and wishing someone to have a good day takes no effort at all, and it can change someone's whole day, even yours.

CHAPTER 7
Obedient

O-be-di-ent: complying or willing to comply with orders or requests; submissive to another's will.

Compliant, acquiescent, tractable, amendable, dutiful, law-abiding, duteous, deferential, unresisting, submissive.

A SCOUT IS OBEDIENT

As mentioned in the definitions, being obedient is complying with requests of others through laws, rules, or tasks given by other people. Obedience can be to yourself as well as to others. It can be as easy as following the speed limit to listening and obeying your scout leaders' orders, and as young boys, staying out of trouble.

I have to say this one might've been tricky at times. When we are young, we are in the learning stage of life. Sometimes we need to break a rule or not follow an order so we learn what punishment can be. It is also the opportunity to realize that following the law or commands is most likely for our benefit. Sometimes it is to test our abilities.

When I was inducted into the Boy Scouts' Order of the Arrow, it came with stipulations and rules to follow. It was a test to see if we could uphold this request and adhere by the rules of the O. A. For Boy Scouts, summer camp is a time to get together, have fun, and learn new things. We always had our summer camp at Camp Buffalo, just outside of Lake Ann. It was a great place to camp, and many scouts from all over the state came to camp there. All day long you worked on merit badges, learning new things that will help you in life, some more than others. I learned a lot of things in scouting that I still use today, more than things I learned in school.

I remember this like it was yesterday. It was a Wednesday afternoon, and the plan was to go to the bowl after dinner for leadership presentations and to participate in sing-alongs. We all lined up and marched down to Grizzly Hall, where all the other scouts were meeting to hike through the woods to a giant hole in the ground they called the bowl. We stood there with respect, saluting the American flag as the color guards of the evening lowered it. When the flag was raised before breakfast, we always said the Pledge of Allegiance. And as it was lowered at night, we respected it with a silent salute as a time we to give thanks to all the men and women who protect our country and that flag. To some it seemed and still seems controversial. I wonder why? Why have they grown to disrespect our flag, the soldiers who fight for it, and the freedoms it brings. People do not understand that the reason they get to speak so freely is because of their freedom.

Bob, a camp supervisor, dismissed the color guards and gave a spiel on how we would all march single file out to the bowl. Then he started dismissing each troop from honors of who was best cheerleaders on our arrival to Grizzly Lodge that evening. We came in third, which out of a dozen troops in camp that week, wasn't half bad. Troop 007 had been the loudest for as long as I could remember, so I wasn't surprised they led the way. Troop 09 was never really a singing group anyway, so being third was kind of impressive.

Singing was the way we showed group cheer. Realize I led these guys to dinner with the only song I knew, the "Marching Ant" song. It was kind of weak, but we sang loudly to make sure we were heard. I know some of you are singing it in your heads now, and others are asking, "What is the 'Marching Ant' song?" Well, to the ones who know it, let's sing:

> The ants go marching one by one, hooray, hooray.
> The ants go marching one by one, hooray, hooray.
> The ants go marching one by one, the little one stops to chew some gum,
> And they all go marching down, into the ground, to get out of the rain.
> The ants go marching two by two, hooray, hooray.
> The ants go marching two by two, hooray, hooray.
> The ants go marching two by two, the little one stops to tie his shoe,

And they all go marching down, into the
ground, to get out of the rain.

Okay, okay. We can stop now. My voice isn't like it used
to be.

As I led our troop through the woods, we told each other
jokes, talked about our day and how much fun we had, and
that we were looking forward to the bonfire we'd have once we
returned to our campsite. But after a while, I realized we made
a wrong turn and wondered why the groups ahead of us were
going down toward the lake instead of up the hill to the bowl.

As we approached the lake, I saw some Native Americans
holding torches. We gathered together, and one of them told
us to be silent. They were all wore what I assumed was war
paint. Being cautious and smart, we went silent as requested.
Once quiet, the Native American who seemed to be in charge
began to read off of a birch bark scroll. He recited a poem
about a chief who traveled across a body of water looking for
warriors. As he read, we saw a canoe lit by a torch floating
across the water. As it got closer, we could see three more
Native Americans. The one in the middle was obviously a
chief as he wore a headdress fit for a chief.

A second canoe made its way around the bend of the
lake and toward. There appeared to be three more Native
Americans in it. Then another for a total of three canoes and
nine more Native Americans. Some of them looked important.
The brave who had spoken to us walked to the shoreline,
pulled the canoes in, and helped the others out. The one I
assumed was the chief walked toward us and looked closely

at us. He nodded and then walked past us. Led by another, they went down a trail followed by the others from the canoes.

The one who spoke to us said we should follow them to a ceremonial dance. Guided by Native Americans, we walked down trails I'd never seen before. They carried torches to light our way. as we came to turns in the path, more Native Americas appeared and dropped in line behind us. Every so often, one let out a yelp or cry. I assumed they were acting like wolves and howling to the moon.

As we walked, we could hear the beat of a drum in the distance. It was faint at first but got louder as we grew nearer. We ended up at the bowl where we were initially heading to, but we showed up from the east instead of from the southwest trail. They escorted us to our seats, and the chief, medicine man, and other higher-up Native Americans I presumed to be the elders, gathered at the bottom. They stood in front of a pile of wood that stood twice the height of the tallest Native Americans standing near it.

Once we all sat down, the chief began to speak, calling on the almighty spirit in the sky to light their fire, be present, and guide them through the ceremony. He went on and on and spoke the names of different braves. Then he asked that the spirit help guide them in their search to find the new warriors for the group before him. As he finished his fire prayer, the sound of thunder roared through the woods and sky. Lightning flashed among the trees, and the gigantic brush and wood pile ignited into flames that easily reached fifty feet into the air. We sat with our mouths open in awe. Some yips and yelps came from the natives all around us. They charged the base of the bowl and began dancing and chanting around the fire, zigzagging and stepping to the beat of the drum repeatedly banging *boom, boom tap, tap boom, boom tap, tap boom, boom tap, tap boom, boom tap, tap boom.* As they danced around the fire, the chief and other elders sat and watched. The drummer began to pick up the pace. The dancers met his beat with every step.

Obedient to the beat, they danced in unison faster and faster, until the beat abruptly stopped. One of the elders got up and walked to the center of the bowl as the dancers cleared the area. Some walked to their posts at the end of each row. Others moved off to the side and circled the fire.

The elder spoke softly as he began his story about two braves who were affectionate toward the same squaw. They had to fight to the death in a dance they called the chicken dance. Another elder walked over to him with a young woman. Two braves stepped forward. Obviously, we were about to witness a dance-off chicken fight thing.

The drum began a slow but steady beat. The braves began to dance and caw around the girl. Every time one screamed out a caw, like a dying bird, the braves changed directions and bumped chests. The drummer quickened the beat, and the two dancers increased their speed and charged each other. They slammed their bodies into each other harder and harder, until finally, one fell and then stumbled back up. And then they did it again until one fell, and exhausted and winded, did not get up. The winner took the girl and walked off. The loser crawled his way off the basin floor to the sidelines and into the woods.

Without missing a beat, the drummer began banging on the drum again. *Boom, boom, boom! Boom, boom, boom, boom!*

Boom! All the dancers started a celebration-style dance around the fire, hooting and cawing and chanting something like, "Eh," or, "Hey," or maybe, "Ah." I wasn't sure, but I thought it was their way to express their cheer.

The dancing and celebration went on for a good forty-five minutes or so. One of the elders came up to us and explained the purposes of the dance. One was for when the braves left their villages to hunt for food. Another was for when they returned.

Finally, it became silent except for the loud popping and snapping of the fire. Then the chief and elders rose from their seats and returned to the center of the ceremonial bowl. The drummer began pounding on the drum with a slow impactful thud. *Boom ... boom ... boom ... boom.* He pounded slow and steady. The chief spoke, and the warriors all yelped and cooed as they ran around and stood ready at the ends of every row of scouts behind us, in front of us, and beside us. They chanted like they were ready for war.

The chief spoke again. This time an elder next to him handed him a birch bark scroll, like the one we saw earlier by the lake. "I say to you, scouts, the spirits have spoken, and your peers have looked upon some of you for guidance. You I call forward are the chosen ones to become warriors with us. As I call your names, you will stand and wait for one of my braves to come and escort you to me. We will exchange words and tap you into our brotherhood."

Chills ran through my bones as I was our senior leader and knew my fellow scouts looked up to me, so the chances of my name being called were highly likely. One by one names were called. Then there it was, "Justen Kayse," my name spoken by the chief. It echoed in my head for a second, like, *Oh my. I can't believe he just said my name.* All my fellow scouts looked at me as I stood.

A brave was to me in a blink of an eye. He grabbed my arm and pulled me to the aisle. Then he ran me down the hill and in front of the elder on the end. Four of them stood there, including the chief and the medicine man. The elder in front of me grabbed my shoulders, squared me up with him, and then asked, "Are you Justen Kayse?" I say yes, and with his hands on my shoulders he raised his left hand and then lowered it down hard on my shoulder. Hard enough I almost flinched. He did this three times. Then he shoved me in front of the next elder of the group. He repeated what the first elder said.

Then he shoved me in front of the chief, who said softly, "So you say you're Justen Kayse. The spirits have called on you. They brought you to us to represent the Order of the Arrow and to be one of us. Do you accept these responsibilities, the tasks, the challenges that lie ahead of you to become one of us?"

My mouth opened and, "I do," came out. The chief tapped my shoulder as the others had. Then he shoved me in front of who I believed to be the medicine man. He looked at me, huffed, and gave me three impactful taps on my shoulders. Then a brave grabbed my arm and pulled me away. He lined me up with the eleven boys who were tapped out before me.

I was the last of the twelve they had chosen, and for me, the night had officially just began. Standing in line and listening to the chief speak to the whole crowd of scouts was exciting and eye-opening as he said they were taking us away and not to worry about our return. *Wait, what? Wait a minute. What did I just agree to? Where are we going?* My mind ran a million miles per hour with questions. As the chief spoke, I started to tune him out with my wild imaginings. Then a brave pushed me to move. The chief and elders were leading us away, with at least a half dozen braves behind us. The drumbeats and dancers were still entertaining the rest of the scouts.

We were led way back into the woods by torch, deeper and deeper into the woods. Eventually, we could no longer hear the beat of the drum, just my heartbeat thumping loud enough for everyone to hear. I didn't know this area of the woods. It was thick and dark. I looked up, and the sky was clear. Millions of twinkling stars lit up the night.

Our walk seemed to take us forever. But as I looked ahead, I finally saw a small light in the distance. As we grew near, I could tell it was a small campfire. A single brave sat there, tending the fire.

The chief motioned us to group around the fire and to sit cross-legged on the ground. When he spoke, he spoke with clarity and passion. You could feel the emotions and sincerity in his voice with every word. We were glued to his words. We listened to story after story from each of the elders around the fire. At the end, we made an oath, a promise, to them. Then the spirits were given. The chief told us, "We will not speak of these events that have gone on or what was said. There will be a vow of silence until the sun rises again." As we got up, the chief added, "Go now with a guide. Sleep well, and remember your promise of obedience to the spirits. It is a promise to yourself. Stay safe, my braves, as you travel in the darkness. Guide them to safety."

A brave walked us into the darkness, away from the fire and down a path that led us by the lake and around to the backside of Grizzly Lodge, where it all began just hours ago. "Here is your lodge. I leave you now, brothers, as you know your way from here. Remember, silence till the sun rises." As the young brave walked away, we all looked at each other, nodded, and walked to our campsites in peace. You could hear everything in the night, from crickets to owls to the laughter of some scouts that were still awake.

I strolled into camp and was immediately bombarded by my fellow scouts, yelling my name at a whisper, "Justen's back. Justen, come here." They all slithered out of their tents to the picnic table, asking question after question. "Where did you go?" "What happened?" "Why is there blood on your face?" I shook my head and used hand gestures to indicate I couldn't speak. I threw my hands up, indicating that I didn't know. Then I turned away and walked to my tent. My hands touched my face, forgetting that there was paint on my forehead. I laid in my bunk and went to sleep.

The next morning, I woke up before the others and beelined it to the shower house to clean up and brush my teeth. I opened the screen door and walked in. It swung shut behind me with a screeching slam. The concrete floor was still wet from the crowd of bathers the night before. I looked in a mirror and saw the war paint on my face. I smiled and stepped out of my clothes and into the cold shower. It was quieter than normal. Being so early, I was the only one there for the first five minutes. It was nice just having water fall over my body, cleansing me from the dirt and whatever was stuck to my face, be it paint or blood.

An oath was taken, and I'll never tell the whole story

of what happened that night. But I will say this: Follow the rules, follow the guidelines given, be true to others as well as yourself, and you will go farther than any other person will.

The shower house was getting loud. It was time for me to get my fellow campers up and moving. I smiled as I toweled off, excited for the day and my new adventure.

As your story unravels from settings to settings, obedience is key to survival and guidance in life. We sometimes take so much for granted that we lose focus on being obedient. That doesn't mean you can't break the rules from time to time as some rules are meant to be broken. But don't be surprised if it doesn't always work out for you when you do. But the key to your success is always to be obedient to yourself. Whatever the cost, be true. I was obedient and followed the rules of the chief because I wanted to grow in the Order of the Arrow. I knew that by following the chief's advice, I'd get there. And I did.

Keeping my silence when I returned only led the younger scouts to ask more questions and increase their curiosity and their drive to be like me so they could be taken away and sworn into a secret organization with only highly honored leaders. If I spoke to them and spilled the beans on everything that happened, some of them would not be interested in going that path. Others would try and cheat their way there. So being obedient to the chief and the oath were key to future leaders.

As this story showed, there are different types of obedience. But each one is for the purpose of greater good. Being obedient helps us to grow internally and externally, depending on what our obedience is for. We can make great strides toward our goals through proper obedience if we follow the rules to get there.

CHAPTER 8

Cheerful

Cheer-ful: noticeably happy and optimistic. Causing happiness by its nature or appearance.

A cheerful person is one full of cheer; in good spirits; a cheerful person. Promoting or inducing cheer; pleasant; bright; cheerful surroundings.

Characterized by or expressive of good spirits or cheerfulness.

A SCOUT IS CHEERFUL

Being cheerful can be contagious. Ultimately, that is the goal of a cheerful person. Spread cheer! When I think of a cheerful person, I think a happy person. I also think my dad was one happy guy. My dad was probably one of the most cheerful people I've ever met. One time his friend, a fellow scouting commissioner, stopped by our house on a Friday afternoon.

He told Dad there was a last-minute overnight scouting trip, and Dad was needed as so many scouts looked to him for his wisdom and perky, cheerful attitude. They knew he was the man to shed some light on their outing.

Mom practically pushed my dad out the door. With an overnight bag and a sleeping bag in hand, they were off. My mom knew what was up as Mr. Olson had called ahead and talked to her.

That weekend turned out to be a camping trip to initiate my dad with the honor of Vigil member of the Order of the Arrow. It is the highest honor an OA member can receive, the elite of the elite in scouting honors. I, being a member of the order, got to hear stories of that night from fellow members and my dad. It sounded like a night to remember.

There are only three membership levels in the OA; I received two of them. Each level has a different initiation ceremony. I was sworn to secrecy never to tell younger scouts how the initiations are done as they may be nominated by their peers to become a member of the OA. I believe I'm safe to tell you all, but just keep it a secret between us.

What my dad didn't know was the adventure he would be going on during a trail hike in the backwoods of Camp Buffalo. He was dropped off in the middle of the backwoods, in the dark. He was given only a few matches and told to keep a fire lit all night long. My dad, being a Boy Scout for so many years and always prepared, was up for the challenge. As the night got darker and time moved on, my dad kept his fire going by keeping it low and small, making it easier to keep going with less wood. As the night grew weary, there was a noise in the distance. It sounded like an owl in the trees just west of where he sat. Then later, from the east, came the sound of rustling in the trees, as though something or someone was walking. Then a voice came from the darkness. "Hey, Mr. Kayse. How are you doing?"

Dad responded with a chipper, "Doing great. Could use some marshmallows or a hot dog though." A laugh came from the darkness and then more rustling in the woods that grew faint as the visitor left the area.

An hour or so passed as my dad sat leaning against a tree, whittling away at a piece of wood he found and whistling a tune. The hoot of an owl chimed in. Dad stopped whistling and called out, "I hear you, old owl, but fear you are no owl. Just a boy with a mission to see if my fire is lit and I am awake. Deepen your voice, son, and your hoot will sound better." The owl sounded again but with a slightly deeper tone. "That's better, young man."

The owl replied, "Thanks, Mr. Kayse," and disappeared into the night.

All night long, the shenanigans continued from various OA members approaching from different directions. If not hooting, they were dancing in the woods and calling out to see how my dad was doing. Sometimes they found him singing and other times whistling or playing his harmonica. And he was always carving away at his new project while keeping his fire lit.

My dad, like others, made it through the night with no issues and entertained the younger OA members who tried to get a rise out of him. One member told me my dad defined cheerfulness to a tee. At no time could they catch or rattle him. And he always put smiles on their faces with his humor, wisdom, and friendly banter.

We choose cheerfulness over all other things to keep our spirits high and hopeful. Being cheerful is part of staying optimistic and bringing hope to you and anyone who surrounds you. Stay cheerful, and your journey through life will be much more pleasant.

CHAPTER 9

Thrifty

Thrift-y: using money and other resources carefully and not being wasteful.

Given to or marked by economy and good management. Thriving by industry and frugality, prosperous.

Synonyms of thrifty: economical, prospering, careful, conserving, flourishing, saving, frugal, industrious, luxuriant, parsimonious, and prosperous.

A SCOUT IS CHEERFUL

Using these words, you'll see that my mother and her seven ways to use a slice a bread was thrifty. I learned to be thrifty from both my parents. When I was little, in our house, bread was also called hot dog buns, hamburger buns, bread pudding, hobo pie crust, and toast. Not to mention it was turkey stuffing and croutons on your salad, Bread is so universal with food that my mom made all kinds of things with it as simple as my PB&J for lunch to dessert, it didn't matter. If we had bread, we had a meal. The money you can save by using bread as multiple things is real dollar bills.

Thrifty comes in many ways, and when it came to scouting, you learned all about making what you have work for you. To be a thrifty scout meant you would be creative and make things work in your favor. If you didn't have a lot of money, you learned to buy what you need and what you can use in multiple ways, like bread. You can use it to make a sandwich but it can be used in all the ways my mother did. Whatever the case, at least you had options.

This also goes for cooking devices. You'd be surprised to learn you can use a frying pan for more than just cooking eggs. I've made chili, burgers, bacon, stir-fry, and steak in a frying pan, so who needs a pot or grill? Thrifty is being thoughtful and creative with what you have. Make the most out of it, and you'll find that creativity can impress you and put a smile on your face.

How else can you be thrifty?

I had an adult leader on a camping trip that showed us all about being thrifty in other ways. On one rainy Saturday— Mr. Coast was his name—taught us how well garbage bags work as rain ponchos. A large trash bag and a knife or scissors, and voilà! A rain poncho so you don't get soaked hiking down the trails or whatever you plan on doing outdoors in the rain.

Some of our most remembered fun adventures were when Mr. Coast was on the camping trips with us. His son Norman was one of my best friends in Boy Scouts, although everyone was my friend in my book. I was a winner when it came to scouting and having so many friends.

One time we camped out in a rustic location. You know, one that you'll hike to out in the middle of nowhere, set up camp, and realize there is no bathrooms for miles. Yep. Oh, no, what will we do? Mr. Coast was the one to show us how handy a shovel can be to dig a hole to use as a bathroom. We even got fancy with it and wrapped a tarp around trees so that we had privacy.

Scouting taught me many things about survival. I'm glad I was in Boy Scouts as school seemed to leave out so many important things you need to learn for adulthood. The merit badges we earned to get to the next rank in scouting taught us about survival, and it gave us insights to the many options to perfect as we got older.

Now all grown up, I still see people being thrifty all the time. I know people who burn wood to heat their homes to save money. We did that as well when I was growing up. I would go out to the woods and cut down dead trees. We would cut them into logs to keep warm in the winter. We didn't have a big, fancy truck that could hold a lot, but I don't think anyone was as creative as my dad at stacking wood on a truck, using branches to create sides, so we could stack above the box's edges. Dad would stack wood higher than the cab of the truck to haul back to the house. He said, "Fewer trips equals less gas used equals saving money for other things."

In my eyes, Dad was an underrated genius. My parents were all kinds of thrifty, from making maple syrup to burning wood for heat. We also had a vegetable garden, and my dad and brother hunted and fished. On our family farm, we raised things like chickens, pigs, turkeys, and a couple cows. one for milk and one for beef. My parents did what they needed to do to live a good life on a budget.

I have friends who still live that type of thrifty lifestyle, raising their kids while teaching them not to be on computers and smartphones that cost money. Instead, to enjoy the outdoors and hunt and fish and learn to be able to live off the land. And most of all, enjoy doing it.

We also have coupons in newspapers and online that we can use to save money. Some people are very thrifty with using coupons, especially on days stores have sales to maximize their savings.

To end this discussion on thriftiness, I can tell you a recent story about a trip to the golf course with friends. I found myself beltless, and by the third hole, I was losing my pants. Luckily, I found a couple pieces of nylon rope, tied them together, and ran my makeshift belt through my belt loops. My friends laughed at me, but I was proud of my ingenuity, creativeness, and ability to solve the problem at hand without going to a store and spending money.

No matter the circumstance, you can find ways to be creative and thrifty. Don't sell yourself short. Sometimes it is fun, especially if you make it profitable. I like to reward myself for my thriftiness with vacations or family road trips. And with a little work and research, you can make them stretch with a little thriftiness as well. Never stop being thrifty.

CHAPTER 10

Brave

Bra-ve: possessing or exhibiting courage or courageous endurance.

Ready to face and endure danger or pain, showing courage without fear.

Having or showing mental or moral strength to face danger, fear, or difficulty; having or showing courage; a brave soldier or a brave smile.

To defy; challenge; dare.

Bold, intrepid, daring, dauntless, heroic.

A SCOUT IS BRAVE

Believe it or not, throughout life our bravery is tested via our skills and what we have accomplished. When it comes to bravery, we test ourselves in many ways. When I got my first tattoo, I was totally testing myself to be brave and strong and handle that needle puncturing my skin over and over for an hour or more straight. Now I can sit for more than three hours getting a tattoo. But that is a tolerance thing at this point.

Being brave is when you are little and riding a bicycle, and your dad takes the training wheels off and pushes you down the driveway. Being brave is going to the big kids' dentist for the first time and sitting still. Being brave is riding your snowmobile over a jump at high speed and catching thirty feet of air. OK, I'm not sure if that is brave or not, but it took guts to do it. Being brave is registering for the draft on your eighteenth birthday, something young adults aren't required to do anymore. Being brave is standing up for what you believe in, not hiding behind others but standing tall and voicing your opinion. Being brave is my brother when he was shipped overseas during the war and served tour after tour, fighting to keep a war off American soil.

Bravery to some is something big. But bravery can be as simple as my daughter getting up the courage to squish a nasty-looking spider on the bathroom wall. That sounds small to me because I grew up camping outdoors and sleeping on the ground with the insects. But for her, it was a mountain to climb, a hurdle to jump, to be brave enough to get close enough she could killed it. For her, she would've rather just torched the house and moved on. I told her she needed to be brave and face her fears; it was the only way to grow and be stronger and braver.

We all have gone through stages of bravery, from our first day leaving our parents to go to preschool or our first time riding a bus by ourselves. Whatever it was, we all encountered

LIV'N THE SCOUT LAW

challenges that tested our bravery skills. I tell you this being brave and facing fears is one of the biggest things that will get you closer to where you want to be. In my daughter's eyes, she was the hero in the story of her killing the spider. After all, she saved the village—our family—from the man-eating spider. For me, she killed a bug. Congrats, and let's move on. But that is because I'd already jumped that hurdle in life. I moved on to the next level in the video game called life.

Picking up a gun and defending your country is a whole different kind can of worms in the bravery category. I bet a lot less of us would do it, not that we don't love our country, but we have a fear of dying that outweighs our bravery. Bravery literally is defeating that big bully called fear. Once we get over fear, nothing can stop us. We are invincible.

During the summer before my freshman year of high school, I worked for Short Lake Township, mowing lawns, doing maintenance, keeping the parks clean and trash picked up, and enjoying the view at the beach on hot summer days. Believe it or not, I loved my job. I was outside every day, getting fresh air and making landscapes look nice.

On a sidenote, my supervisor was also my elementary school librarian, which was kind of funny to me. She is a great lady and a volunteer firefighter on top of everything. It takes a lot of courage and bravery to be willing to run into a burning building. So many times you see most people run from danger, and first responders run to it. They have conquered a totally different level of bravery.

But that wasn't what I wanted to talk about. And it wasn't even about how good I was at cutting grass around those gravestones in the cemeteries. I wanted to about the township's association with a Grow Better young adult program. That meant I was a part of it, and this program helped us in some of our weaker areas. For example, I was sent to an education lab to improve my English—I still speak and write below average—as well as my computer skills, though I still peck at the keys. But the other thing we had to do was an overnight strength camp thing. It was a total game-changer in trust, bravery, obedience, kindness, cheerfulness, and being helpful. It wasn't any part of scouting, but there are pieces of the Boy Scout law, showing you it is important in everyone's lives to have these skills and to grow with them.

In this program, we were required to learn about someone else at the event, which just happened to be your bunkmate. My bunkmate was Sal. He was a cool dude and kind of quiet. But once we got to know each other, I grew another level of respect for him, especially when it came to what our days ahead were going to teach us. We did a nature walk. As a teen, it was boring, but as we walked, we stopped and listened to a counselor/guide talk about different things, like obstacles and how to overcome them. One of the stops was standing on a platform fastened to a tree a good thirty-six inches off the ground. We had to face the tree and fall backward into the group's hands, trusting them to catch us. It is called a trust fall, and the object was to trust them to catch you. The more you trusted them, the more you stood up straight and fell freely. I'm not gonna lie; I didn't know these people. We all came from different jobs and different walks of life. But to do this, to put your life and well-being into someone else's hands, was a big deal. You must create some sort of bravery to be able to do a trust fall. Yes, I slightly bent my knees, and I believe everyone did to some degree.

They also had us do a balancing beam walk. It was only six inches off the ground, but it taught us slow and steady can get the job done. Then there was another one, twelve inches off the ground. A little more bravery was needed for that one. And finally, there was one was two feet off the ground and ten feet long.

They had things we did by ourselves, like going over six-foot walls, and then as a team, going over ten-foot walls. There were challenges for which we needed a partner, liking walking tightropes that were only a foot off the ground. It was a fun day, and we all had laughs and stories to tell at a campfire that night. That made me feel right at home, being a Boy Scout and all. I learned Sal was a Boy Scout in Cadillac, so it was nothing new for him either.

Our counselors told us that day was preparation for the next day, and that was what life is about. What we do today should prepare us for something bigger in the future. We had no idea what was in store for us, but the anticipation was enough to keep us awake half the night. (And bonus, we were still getting paid.)

The next morning, we grabbed breakfast and took a walk, talking about the building blocks of our lives and career paths. It was about taking challenges head-on, like a thirty-foot climbing wall that stood in front of us.

We all took deep breaths. Chills ran up and down our spines as the counselors told us how this challenge was going to work. After you climbed the wall, which probably to all of us was a huge accomplishment on its own, but then you had to come down. The counselor turned and pointed way over on the other side of the woods. We looked above us and saw ropes tied from tree to tree, each with different challenges, like the things we did the day before. But this time, they were all more than thirty feet in the air. I might've looked brave on the outside, but at that moment, I was very nervous.

Now, I grew up in the country and on a family farm, and climbing trees was like a hobby of mine. So it was exciting for me to climb and conquer that wall. But the fact was, heights are not my strong suite. To be honest, I didn't get nervous until I got to the top of the wall and looked down.

My confidence was strong when it came to strapping on a harness and climbing that wall in record time. My partner, not as much. But because I jumped at the chance to get up there, he had to follow.

The climb was exciting; the wall was no match for a monkey like me, so it didn't take long. My adrenaline was pumping by the time I got to the top and met the first of many guides up in the trees. The problem was when I turned and looked down. Never look down! In life, we tend to look back at where we came from, and that can muddy the water and confuse us. Me looking down after that climb made me freeze. I was in no shape to move as my fear of heights just got real. I think I turned red in fear of falling, even though I was strapped into a harness tethered to a cable fastened to a tree. My newfound friends were at the bottom to catch me if I fell, right? I mean we did practice a trust fall and all. I was still very scared and did not want to move on.

It took a little coaching to getting me to relax and move across the platform to the next challenge, but finally, after hours (OK, minutes that seemed like hours), I moved to the next challenge it was simple a walk in the park across a high wire only ten feet long. Not bad. I was proud of myself and how brave I became after each obstacle.

Even though it took Sal a little more time to get up the wall, he never looked down and was right behind me, moving right along. He even talked me through some challenges. In fact, at one point, I think he passed me somewhere, somehow.

There were all kinds of challenges, including a cargo net climb, wobbly tightropes, and a V shape of tightropes. In the latter one, you had to press your hands against your partner's and keep stepping sideways to the other side. At one point, we were pushing on each other so hard to not fall as we scooted to the other side facing the ground. It was scary as we went inch by inch, hoping the other person would stay strong. That was when we were at our widest point. Our hands were sweaty, and we kept slipping until we fell. Thank God for harnesses. The fall was literally like a foot or two, but then we were just hanging there in midair, laughing now that we knew we were not gonna die.

After many challenges and obstacles, we finally came to the end, successful at all but one, which gave us more confidence. After the fall, we became fearless with other obstacles knowing the fall wasn't so bad. We got to the end and zip-lined to the ground in yippee fashion. It was a blast!

All of us learned being brave and facing our fears was challenging, but the journey was fun and rewarding. Being brave enough to complete a task proves you can grow, and you get rewarded for that bravery.

CHAPTER 11

Clean

Clean: free from dirt, marks, or stains.

Morally uncontaminated; pure; innocent: clean living.

A SCOUT IS CLEAN

Being clean may be hard work. We all like to get a little dirty when we play. Luckily for us, this clean has a little more depth to it than just keeping our bodies and clothing clean.

In 1988, a few of us were able to go to the national jamboree. It was one of the largest gatherings of scouts from across the United States. Even a few were there from other countries. We set up camp at a military base in Virginia. This place was huge, my first time—but not my last—on a military base, and my first time to leave Michigan.

There were all kinds of things to do and scouts to meet. One of the things we could do was an obstacle course. Goggles were highly recommended as when kids came off this course, they were drenched in mud from head to toe. Talk about *not* being clean. So if we're talking about physically clean, we would fail miserably.

Have you ever heard the phrase "clean living"? We can explain clean better by talking about living a clean-living life. You ask, "How you do that?" Well, the easiest way for me to explain would be to tell you about some friends of our family. If you drive down North Short Lake Road, past the little party store, up the hill, and follow the stone wall around the corner, it wraps around right into a dirt driveway that leads to a little white house on the hill. This is the home of Mr. and Mrs. Hoffman. I was only a small boy when I knew the Hoffmans, but they demonstrated what clean living was all about, even to a young boy.

No matter what time we showed up at their house, it was always just in time for an apple pie or a crumb cake to be coming out of the oven. And no, we didn't try to time it that way. Mrs. Hoffman was so kind to always offer us some dessert and conversation. It was like going to the library and having a book read to you; everyone listened.

Mr. Hoffman was a tall, slender man who reminded me of the sixteenth president, Abraham Lincoln. He always seemed to have a smile on his face, half the size as his wife's smile, but it was always there. It didn't matter what it was, he was always willing to help a neighbor, even if that neighbor lived two miles away, like we did. The man was no mechanic but was never afraid to roll up his sleeves and help work on a car, build a barn, whatever you needed. If he was available, he was there.

They brought fresh vegetables they grew to the church.

They'd always tell you, "Oh, we have way too much, and it'll just go to waste if someone doesn't take it."

They always respected everyone they met. They were and so pure in a sense. In fact, "genuine" is the word I'm looking for. And a pleasure to be around anytime.

I don't remember, but my parents told me Mr. Hoffman stepped up at church and gave the sermon because we lost our pastor. I guess he ended up serving as the pastor for over ten years, until the church found a new one.

He wasn't afraid to do anything and was always honest. One spring he even came to our farm and helped us make maple syrup. He told us he knew nothing about it except that it tasted good on Mrs. Hoffman's pancakes. But show him what to do, and he would lend a hand. That could mean going into the woods on a snowmobile with a sled in tow, carrying fifty-gallon barrels for pouring sap into. As the snow melted, we'd use a truck to gather the sap, but most of the time, we did it all on our 1968 Boa Ski snowmobiles. We drove tree to tree, emptying buckets of sap into the barrel till it was close to full.

Then we went back to the sap house to put it into the large water tank we had at the end of the sap house. The process of making maple syrup was long. Collecting the sap was just the beginning. You have to boil down the sap until it becomes syrup. We did this in an eight-foot by four-foot pan over a large fire. All through the night, someone had to stoke the fire and add more sap as needed. It would take days to get a batch of golden-brown pure maple syrup ready. My mom was always the taste tester to judge if it was ready. And when it was, she let everyone else have a taste to concur with her that it was time to pull the pan off the fire and bottle the syrup.

When Mr. Hoffman got to taste it for the first time, his face lit up with the biggest smile I'd ever seen. I tell you, some of the best times were the stories told during maple syrup season. I could go on and on about making maple syrup and how my sister Jean and I always wanted to stay up to help even on school nights. We never wanted to miss the taste-testing. But we must continue.

Being clean is truly about following the Boy Scout law, having respect for others, and being honest with them and yourself, and enjoy doing it. As long as you were, and you followed simple hygiene, I think you were pretty clean.

CHAPTER 12

Reverent

Rev-er-ent: feeling or showing deep and solemn respect.

Being reverent is feeling awe and respect. Someone who constantly gives thanks and praise to God.

When you have great awe and respect for someone or something, and you show it by respectfully worshipping that person, thing, deity, or musical group, you are being reverent.

Synonyms for reverent are respectful, adoring, worship, venerating, solemn, devout, dutiful, humble, religious, and godly.

A SCOUT IS REVERENT

Ideally, when they hear the word "reverent," they immediately think godly thoughts. And they have a form of worship, prayer, love, and peace with their inner selves, as well as faith in a larger dimension spiritually.

Reverence means something different to everyone. Some of us are reverent to a higher being; some are gods, and some are not. I'm here to say stay passionate about being reverent in your own way. We all need this in our lives, but as you'll read in this chapter, I focus on my reverence to a Christian God. It wasn't always easy and I'd be lying if I didn't say I lost my way once or twice through the years. I believe it is okay to do so as it is a test of our growth, development, and direction in lives.

Let me begin with my childhood and how I felt as a young boy being dragged to church on a sunny Sunday when the fish were biting. I went, oh, yes, kicking and screaming like most boys my age, believing I was being punished for considering having fun on the lake instead of learning and worshipping our God inside four walls on a hilltop overlooking the lake that called my name.

You might ask, "Why did you feel like you were being punished?" I preferred to be doing things I understood. Sitting quietly in a church, listening to someone speak in a foreign language, did nothing for me. No, they didn't really speak a foreign language, but to me, everything they spoke was Greek, and I'm not Greek. I now understand it was my mother trying to share something she loved to do and believed in with her children. Church was important to my mother, and she wanted it to be important to us kids as well. It only took thirty years, but I get it now. Thanks, Mom.

As I sit here today, I can tell you a preacher, a pastor, a bishop, a cardinal, a monk, or whoever stands before you to preach the Word of God is a storyteller. They must do so in a way that you'll relate to and understand it. Trust me when I say I've stood or sat in front of many and didn't understand any of them. And if you don't speak to me so I understand, then I'm not interested in learning. So is it any surprise I drifted away from a godly state of reverence? Not at all. Surprisingly enough, it happens to many people.

Nowadays, reverence is referred to in a broader sense because so many people respect or idolize more things, more people, as well as other spiritual beings than just the God I speak of. God for some is different than for others. I have friends I went to high school with in Cadillac, Michigan, are very reverent to the music they listen to, and the respect they show for their band idols is almost a religion. For some of them, it is. I love seeing people with such deep emotion and love for things. Even if it's not what I find reverent, it is important to them, and I respect that.

I was brought up in a house of God, and believe it or not, like I said earlier, I was the little boy who was kicking and screaming every Sunday as I was dragged to church by my collar. I by no means was a perfect child like you all think I was. (I know it's hard to believe, but just ask my sister.) Sitting in church as a little boy on a Sunday was not the ideal thing. No matter how you twisted the story, it was boring. I can imagine that almost every little boy and girl who went to church would agree with me.

I grew up in a typical or nontypical church, depending on who you were. In fact, I grew up going to Short Lake Friends Church, a Quaker church just outside of Cadillac, Michigan. With a small congregation, it was one of those places where everyone knew your name.

As I have mentioned several times already, I despised going to church when I was a boy. I even didn't like going to Bible school in the summer. It was always a struggle for me to understand it. It wasn't that I was a bad kid, it was just not explained to me in a language I, a child, understood, so I grew to hate it. Let's get this straight: I hated going to church, not God. In my eyes, church was for grown-ups, and maybe someday, once I was an adult, I'd understand it and grow to like it. But as a boy, it was not my cup of tea.

As I got older, it still didn't grow on me. But it was part of scouting, so I accepted it as that. I didn't mind going, and I sometimes understood little bits and pieces of it. And at times, I was thinking of other things. OK, I was a teenager, so I was thinking about girls. My mind wandered—a lot—and maybe, just maybe that was part of the problem.

Church at camp was held outside. The pastor kept scouting relevant to his stories about God, and I understood them more clearly. My mother, on the other hand, was a great example of a true Christian heart, and I'd say very reverent to her Christianity. She went to church faithfully and always leant a helping hand in the kitchen on potluck Sundays. She believed in bringing the family and making sure we respected the church and its members. Unless my mom was sick, she was always in church on Sunday, and she lived her life following the Word of God, respecting him and the written Word of the Bible. My respect for my mother's devotion to Christ and being such a great role model in that aspect is high. I love her for showing me that passion. I always try to raise my standards to match my mom's and dad's, but it will be a goal I will always chase. And I'm fine with that.

If you tell me some of the other meanings of the word "reverent," like respect, then I can easily relate to and do that. And if you say it is to be in awe of something, well, I can very much be in awe. So being reverent in scouting wasn't necessarily as hard as being a little boy going to church and falling asleep in the back pew. No, it was different. Being reverent in scouting was more understandable.

As we grow in life, I believe we grow in our reverence because we understand more as we get older. I write this as a student of God, not as a master who knows all by any means. When I go to bed, I pray to God because that is what I believe in. I ask God to help me daily, and when others need help, I ask God to help them and guide them and comfort them in their times of need. I don't think twice about it.

I'm not perfect. Nor am I the guy you see in church every Sunday. But there are so many churches out there now and some that I can actually relate to and understand. I'm an adult now, so it is easier for me to understand the big words and to be reverent in this fashion. My faith grows every day, and the miracles I've seen will hold my faith solid. Even though I may not seek God in a church, I find him everywhere I go. The advancement in technology in today's world gives you the Word of God at your fingertips.

We all have our vices and what we believe and worship. To me, that is okay as I believe we all just need guidance of some kind that is outside our realms. Whether it be my God or your spiritual belief, it doesn't matter. Believe, respect, and worship at your own will to whoever you want.

For me, I need to have my dose of gratitude, so my reverence to God aligns me to give him my gratitude. With so many beliefs in today's world we, can choose to who or what we give our reverence, as well as our gratitude. My words to you are this: Just make sure you do it as it will ease stress, among other things, from your mind. Your mind will be opened for more productive thoughts.

One more thing before I leave you in this chapter. My belief in God—whether it is in a church or in the great outdoors, wherever I may be—is based in respect. I'm in awe of what he can do and what miracles he has showed me. You ask what miracles? Yes, my beliefs came full circle; I will explain the miracle he blessed me with in another book. His power is so great and wonderful. You'll be in awe when it hits you. And that, my friends, is reverence.

CHAPTER 13

And Always Hungry

Hun-gry: feeling or displaying the need for food; having a strong desire or craving.

A SCOUT IS HUNGRY

Well, to be fair, if you look up the Boy Scout law, you will not find hungry in there anywhere. But if you ask any scout, he will surely tell you hungry is a part of it. Otherwise, we'd all starve. I tell you, this boy has got to eat! Boy Scouts can be a lot of work, and boys tend to work up appetites. They love when it is chow time.

But let's be honest. I'm talking about the urge, the desire, the craving to expand our minds and our bodies to do more with life than just the norm. When we all spent our summers at Camp Buffalo, I guarantee we all knew where Grizzly Hall was and when it was feeding time. Breakfast, lunch, or dinner, you could hear the roar of scouts conversing at the lodge. The real hunger was not in our bellies, even though we were there to fill them up, our hunger was to learn new things and grow to be better people. That never goes away unless something major, like a disaster, occurs and takes the wind out of our sails and sinks our boats. But that is a story for another time and another book.

We crave to be better. We look for ways to advance ourselves to be more and to make more. As a Boy Scout, that was obvious. If you wanted a higher rank, you had to get more merit badges and pass different tests. But that Eagle at the top of the totem pole is what every boy wanted. It meant we had to have ambition, a drive to get it, a hunger; we had to be hungry for success. It all depends on how hungry you are to get there. I was hungry. I wanted it all. And I not only made it to the highest rank in Boy Scouts—the Eagle—I went farther and higher as there was more to learn and more to get. I wanted more.

In life we want that too. You look at a billionaire and wonder why he wants all that money. What is he or she going to do with it all? They can't possibly spend it all. The answer to those questions is that it's not about the money. It's about your freedom. Yes, your hunger for one thing leads to another. And by the end of it all, it is for your freedom to do whatever you want.

When you add hunger to the equation, you multiply everything you do. When I was a young adult, I someone once told me the one who dies with the most toys wins. I thought, *Well, I better go out and get a boat and a car and a truck and a motorcycle and a snowmobile and a four-wheeler.* And I did. I was killing this thing, and when I die, people are going to think, *Wow, he had a lot of stuff!* I was hungry to get more all the time.

I can tell you, however, it really isn't about who dies with the most toys. It's so much more than that, which I'll explain in more detail in my next book.

I cannot tell a lie as a scout who is also hungry as well as abides by the previous twelve scout laws. I figured as a bonus, I'd throw in that every scout on Planet Earth agrees that always hungry should definitely be added as the thirteenth law. Obviously, if I haven't been clear enough on being hungry, to be hungry is the *want* to grow, to learn, and to expand your knowledge and well-being for a better life. Simply put, wanting more.

CONCLUSION

I lie here, awake at 11:30 at night, staring at the ceiling, wondering how I should end this book. How do I follow the Boy Scout laws with a closing to make you realize these words are not only for me and you but for every person out there who wants to learn and live better lives?

Some of you are scouts, and some of you were scouts. And others never were scouts, but you picked this book up to see what scouts learned and if you missed out on anything. Or maybe you were a scout and needed to dust off the boots and have a refresher, a reminder of how you should live, and some guidance to get back on track. We are not perfect; we stray sometimes. But if we remind ourselves of these laws, we can regroup and conquer anything in our paths.

Believe me, there are more things to learn and more things for me to say. This is not the end of Boy Scout training. I promised you in the beginning that there would be more, and the scout promise and motto are in my second book. If you want more answers and guidance, if you learned anything from this book, the next one is a nail-biter. And if you think this book helped, hands down you need the next book as it will catapult you into growth. I will not leave you with just a referral to read more of my books, but if you need anything like books, motivation, and a list of all the great people who motivate me, please follow me on Instagram, YouTube, and Facebook. Check out my website for any updates or new book releases.

But more important let's finish this strong with hunger for more. I can tell you that as a young man, I grew hungry for success. And when I learned how to spell entrepreneur, I was hooked. I was thirsty for more, and slowly but surely, I grew hungrier with every bite of wisdom I learned. I could be more and wanted more. I saw a meme on social media that said it best: "If you can dream it, you can do it." I love that statement and everything that comes with it because it means I'm unstoppable.

When I started golfing, I golfed left-handed. Yep, I did. Why? Because I'm left-handed. Duh! More important, I was bad at golf, but I had friends who liked golf, and in some weird way, I did too. I worked with a buddy named Antonio. He was a good golfer, played on the school golf team, and all. He put a right-handed club in my hand, and the rest, they say, is history. My hunger for the game grew. I've been playing golf for a long time, and I'm always getting better. Now I'm an assistant pro, teaching golf. I'm at a level that I'm trying to get certified because my hunger is strong, and I refuse to quit. I learned one thing: Use the laws of scouting and go after your dreams till you can check them off your list. I hope you have that same hunger and plan to one day check your dreams off your list.

As you've read this book, you'll have noticed that the Boy Scout law is the *foundation* of everything you do. It is truly a building block to a successful life. It doesn't matter who you are or what you do, if you are a parking lot attendant or a doctor, the base to your life's goals is the same. So go out, and put the laws of scouting to work for you. Do what you love, and most of all, be happy.

"Wait, what about all those famous people you mentioned in the beginning of the book?" you ask. "No examples on how they made it work for them?" Ahh, I leave that for you to uncover and realize. You see, we must uncover some mysteries on our own. That is how the Boy Scout law works. We learn it, we use it, and we discover how others use it. Then we can perfect it to fit our needs and help us rise us to the top of our ladders and receive our goals and dreams. We run our own races, and only we can cross the finish line and win the awards for ourselves. We can look at others as examples of how they became successful, but our journeys will be down our own paths, dealing with our own roadblocks.

Let me leave you with this. Believe it or not, M. J. was rejected as a basketball player and told to do something else. But he was brave and kept trying. He was loyal to his passion and never quit using that rejection as fuel to not only succeed but to become the best basketball player ever. Michael stayed hungry and obedient to his craft. He strove to become the best and to help his team become champions. Now it is time for you to build the foundation and make your dreams come true.

Trustworthy

Trust is when you have faith in the bridge that you cross that someone else built.

Loyal

A dog is loyal to the one who feeds him.

Helpful

Helping others is as simple
as lending a smile when you
see someone without one.

Friendly

Being friendly creates positive connections that turn into friendships.

Courteous

*It's simple acts of kindness
with the expectation of
receiving nothing in return.*

Kind

Be kinder than expected.

Obedient

Obedience is the tightrope between your goals and your accomplishments.

Cheerful

A cheerful person is one who can express the happiness he or she feels inside.

Thrifty

*A penny in your pocket is
a penny not spent.*

Brave

Be brave, and go where you've never been. It could be the greatest adventure you'll ever take.

Clean

If we do right by ourselves,
we will never be dirty.

Reverent

Believing in the power of a greater being and having faith will bring you happiness.

Hungry

You have to be so hungry
that you can taste victory
before you even start.

ABOUT THE AUTHOR

Justen A. Kayse was born and raised in the cherry capital of Michigan. He is the youngest of eight children and the entrepreneur of the family. He still lives a Scout's life, helping others and chasing dreams. He spends his free time talking to his dog in many voices, telling her lame jokes as he thinks up new ideas to make the world a better place.

CPSIA information can be obtained
at www.ICGtesting.com
Printed in the USA
JSHW022318270423
40861JS00001B/101